FULWELL
Home to Trams, Trolleys and Buses

Professor Bryan Woodriff

MP *Middleton Press*

Cover pictures:

Front upper: *The final assembly and fitting out of the Feltham cars was undertaken at Fulwell Depot.*

Front lower: *Six new trolleybuses - Nos. 160, 164, 167 etc. wait on the Stanley Road apron in 1935. Note that the traction poles still retain their finials and decorative bases. An old Diddler is nose to the wall in the background.*

Rear upper: *The author was recorded, when Deputy Mayor of Richmond 1986-7, at the controls of the preserved Feltham Tramcar no. 355 in the London Transport Museum at Covent Garden.*

Rear lower: *Dennis DT 73 on route 33 emerges from the Wellington Road forecourt with the Controllers' 'cosy' little Box on the left. It was later destroyed when hit by a bus and all its equipment was crushed.*

**Published to commemorate the
centenary of Fulwell Depot
in 2003.**

Published July 2003

ISBN 1 904474 11 X

© *Middleton Press, 2003*

Design   *Deborah Esher*
              Dvaid Pede

Published by
          Middleton Press
          Easebourne Lane
          Midhurst, West Sussex
          GU29 9AZ

Tel: 01730 813169
Fax: 01730 812601
Email: enquiries@middletonpress.fsnet.co.uk

Printed & bound by Biddles Ltd, Kings Lynn

CONTENTS

INTRODUCTION AND ACKNOWLEDGEMENTS

From the start, Fulwell Depot has always been known as the friendly 'family depot'. Generations of the same family have found employment in this tram, trolleybus and bus garage and have created a remarkably friendly atmosphere which is still demonstrated by the retired transport workers and their spouses who meet regularly in the Club and Institute building which Clifton Robinson created at the same time the great LUET tram-shed and associated buildings were being erected. It has been used for many recreational and educational activities in its time. The acronym 'LUET' is also Latin and means, 'Let there be light'. The illuminating story of Fulwell is intimately bound up with the 'Hampton Court loop via Teddington and via Hampton'.

With rationalisation and, over the years, the closure of some bus garages in west London, retired transport personnel have continued to find comradeship and friendly support at Fulwell. It is to them and those who preceded them in the provision of a first class service of public transport in south Middlesex and north Surrey that this volume of reminiscences is dedicated.

For their sponsorship and co-operation I would like to thank both London United Busways: Alex Juniper, Michael Foster, the AVL & Output Dept. **and** Tellings-Golden Miller: Bill Hiron, Glenn Jenkins and Mary Dunne; for their support and help - the members of Fulwell Club and Institute: Pat Piggott, Peter Butler, George Pike, Lorna Cassidy, Jack Clements, Arthur Williams, Bill Cleeson, Mrs Gubbins, Denis Boyd, Sue Kenyon and many more; London's Transport Museum at Covent Garden: Oliver Green, Hugh Robertson and Simon Murphy; the Bristol Record Office: John Wilson; the National Tramway Museum, Crich: Rosie Thacker (Dr Hugh Nicol) and Cyril Smeeton of LRTA; the London Borough of Richmond upon Thames Local Studies Collection: Jane Baxter; the LBRuT Department of Planning, Transport & Client Services: David Stabb and Russell Morris; David Allen - R&TT, John's Place - Hampton Hill, Hampton Hill Hardware, John Inglis - Hampton-online, Ron Keevil, Nancy Shepherd, David King, John Sheaf, Geoffrey Wilson and John Woodriff.

I must also thank Malcolm Claridge who has been an enormous help finding so many bus photographs and providing suitable captions and Godfrey Croughton for the tickets.

I owe a special debt of gratitude to Mr George Gundry of Wimbledon and Mrs Elizabeth Seal of Norbiton who encouraged my interest in the London United Electric Tramways as long ago as 1966 when I celebrated at Kingston College of Technology the 60th Anniversary of the first tramcar across the Thames with an exhibition of artefacts, models and historic photographs.

1. HISTORICAL AND GEOGRAPHICAL SETTING

In 1894, James Clifton Robinson, the general manager and engineer of the Bristol Tramways Company, together with other directors and colleagues, acquired and refurbished the dilapidated West Metropolitan Tramways Company's horse-drawn system between Shepherds Bush and Acton, and between Hammersmith Broadway, Chiswick and Kew Bridge.   They renamed it London United Tramways Limited.   However, it was not the intention of the new directors to simply run an efficient but small horse-drawn tramway. They were determined to provide the suburbs of west London with a comprehensive system of electric tramways which would be the model and example not just for the capital but for the rest of the country.

An Act of Parliament was obtained in 1895 which conditionally gave the Company powers to install electric traction but, although the London County Council and other local bodies such as Ealing refused their permission, Clifton Robinson appealed directly to the ratepayers with a pamphlet, "The Case for the Trams" and eventually won consent.   Similar battles were fought and won at Twickenham, Hampton, Hampton Wick and Kingston with only Teddington showing a degree of willingness to co-operate with the new tramway through its Tramway Committee.

Sir James Clifton Robinson (1848-1910) developed from the age of 12 a great interest in the promotion, construction and management of tramways both at home and abroad. His sound knowledge aided his promotion to Managing Director of the Imperial Tramways Company Limited and he used his engineering skills to improve old tramways and develop new ones. Robinson was smitten by the power of electric traction and he resolved to electrify the new tram routes his Company - London United - proposed for west London. He chose to live in Hampton at Garrick's Villa and had his own private line into the grounds.   In January 1910, after discussion with the sister company, the Underground Electric Railways Company of London, Robinson resigned.   In the November of that year, while in New York with his wife, he fell ill on a tramcar and died in a nearby chemist's store a short time afterwards.

By 1901 the Company had won the consent of almost all the local authorities through which it wanted to run its electric tramway although it had not yet begun to electrify any of the lines it already operated.   One major obstacle was the Royal Observatory at Kew where it was thought that the electric current might affect the recording of observations of the variation of the earth's magnetic field.   The problem was solved by the Company paying most of the costs to transfer the Observatory to Eskdalemuir in Scotland.   In the meanwhile, Clifton Robinson and his staff had been busy erecting poles, fitting wires, re-laying the tracks, building a power station on the Chiswick High Road and purchasing new electric tramcars so that electric trams were seen running for the first time through London's streets on 4th April 1901 from Hammersmith to Kew Bridge, from Acton to Shepherd's Bush. Chiswick, with its new power station and a tall graceful chimney, new tram sheds and offices, became the local headquarters of the company but it was soon realised that if it were to fulfil Sir Clifton Robinson's dreams of a vast tramway empire in south Middlesex and north Surrey, it did not have enough capacity to provide and maintain an expanded regular service through Hounslow to Twickenham, Hampton Court and beyond.

A new large tram shed would have to be built and several sites were investigated. Already the LUT was planning its new lines towards Hampton Court and when the southerly part of the Freake Estate by South Road in Teddington became available on the death of the Dowager Lady Freake in 1901, Clifton Robinson entered into difficult negotiations with the Trustees of the Estate and eventually secured a 99 year lease for the Fulwell land on which to construct his massive tramcar depot at an annual rent of £200. For many years Sir Charles and Lady Freake had occupied the Lodge at Fulwell Park just south of the River Crane.

Sir Clifton Robinson wanted the new Fulwell depot to be large enough to cope with all the tramcars he would need for the new lines he proposed or had permission to construct to Hampton Court, to Kingston and Wimbledon via the Dittons and from Hampton Court via Sunbury to Staines.   No sooner had he acquired the agreement in April 1902 than he began construction of the Fulwell sub-station and to lay out the lines in the open fields. The site was not quite rectangular because the LSWR approaches to Fulwell station sliced through the SE corner giving the ground a skewed appearance from Wellington Road in the west through to Stanley Road in the east.   The Depot was built on the grand scale. It had 18 tracks of which 15 were available for through running from either end of the building. To the south there were three extra tracks from the Wellington Road end but, because of the kink in the shed at this point, they stopped short of the Stanley Road end, had no exit to Stanley Road, and became the Repair Shop. Both ends of the depot had four gabled and pedimented spans, the northerly three of which each gave access to five through tram tracks. Clerestories capped the lofty roofs of all four bays at the top of which were glazed circular windows except the second from the left at both ends where a large clock was installed. The depot was finished by the end of March 1903 and on 2nd April , the tramway to Hampton Court was inaugurated from Stanley Road via Teddington and Hampton Wick. Two days later the trams began the service to Hampton Court via Hampton Hill and Hampton on what was to be called the 'Hampton Court Loop'. The fascinating story of the Fulwell Depot had begun to unfold.

1.1   Alderman Judge, Mayor of Kingston, at the controls of the replica tram in the 1966 Exhibition.

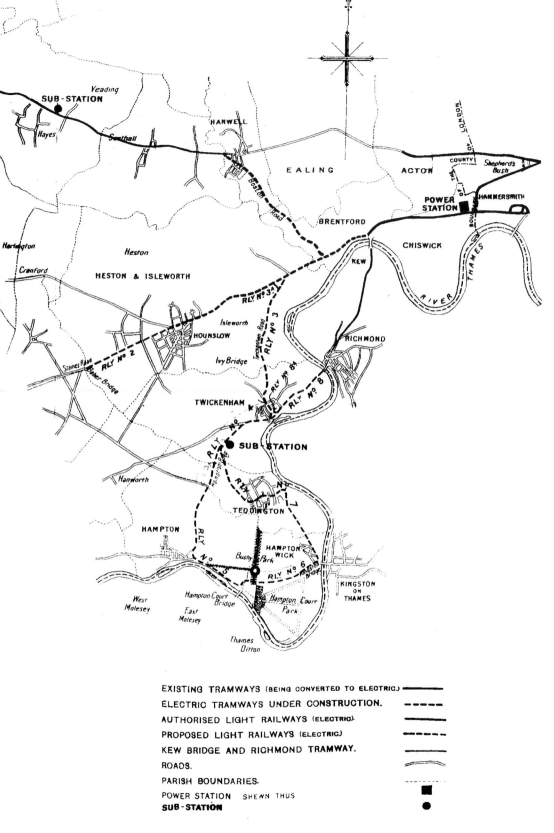

1.2   Map of actual and proposed routes in 1899.

1.3   An early LUET car stands at Kew Bridge with the Pumping House Tower in the background.

1.4   Robinson's drawing of the prototype of the open topped tramcar.

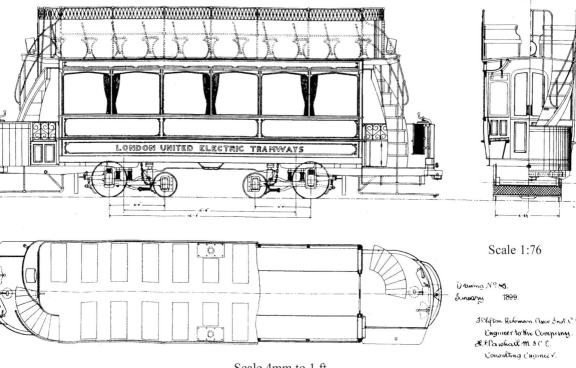

Scale 1:76

Drawing N° 45.
January   1899.

J Clifton Robinson Assoc Inst C° E
Engineer to the Company.
R Harwall M I C E.
Consulting Engineer.

Scale 4mm to 1 ft.

1.5   The new Chiswick Power Station, 16th October 1900.

1.6   The Chiswick Tram Depot, 27th December 1900.

1.7 The Tramway Company's workforce lay the wooden blocks (9ins x 3ins x 4½ inches) to create a perfect roadway near Twickenham Green - to everyone's advantage!

1.8 Pushing ahead towards Fulwell, the road has to be levelled, the track laid and the blocks inserted to the required standard.

2. BUILDING OF THE TRAM SHED AND DEPOT

2.1 Still there today, the houses in South Road pinpoint the location of the Freake's land which was leased to the tramway company for its depot in 1902. Work has begun in earnest to level the site.

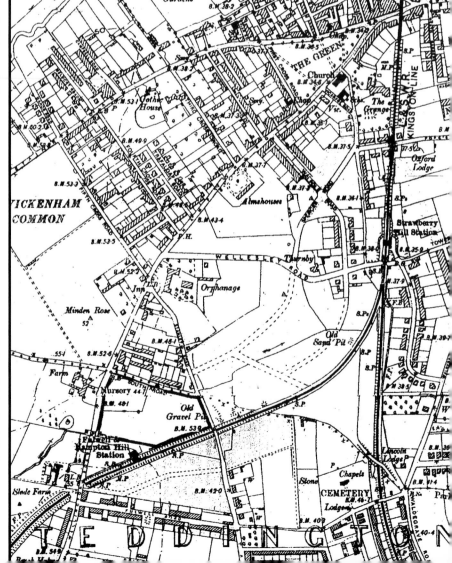

2.2 Map of the site in 1900 at the scale of 6 ins to 1 mile. The creation of a triangular railway junction nearby is described in *Kingston and Hounslow Loops (Middleton Press)*.

2.3   The main pair of tramlines has been laid from the rise in Stanley Road through to the opposite end of the site at Wellington Road.   In the distance on the left, the new substation is being built and on the right, the new office complex.

2.4   The track has been laid on the left up the rise of Stanley Road to the railway bridge over the London and South Western Railway.

2.5   The old bridge in Stanley Road over the railway line is seen in 1902.

2.6   The new bridge capable of supporting the tramway to Teddington over the cutting of the LSWR line approach to Fulwell station.

2.7   From the Wellington Road end the depot tracks fan out into their respective bays while the depot is being built around them.

2.8   The substation building nears completion and the five tracks of the depot fan give a good idea of how the lines were laid and fixed.

2.9   Laying the lines in a very narrow Wellington Road past the sub station towards Hampton Hill.

Teddington Urban District Council.

Report of the Tramways Sub-Committee.

Your Sub-Committee have to report that they met Mr. Clifton Robinson, the Managing Director to the London United Tramways, Limited, Mr. Holmes, Assistant Engineer, and Mr. Roberts, representing the Solicitors to the Company, on the 2nd May, and, subject to your approval, recommend :—

1.—That the plans as submitted to you having been amended and brought into conformity with the deposited plans be approved/subject to the hereinafter mentioned conditions, viz., that the approval is not to bind the Council as to the position of the poles and cableways.

2.10   Joining the main track in Wellington Road to the depot track fan just in front of the substation.

2.11   The finished entrance to the depot from Wellington Road, showing how the jarrah wood setts have been fixed in place.   The original office block is behind the fine brick wall on the left.

2.12   A view of the electricity generator in the substation at Fulwell.

2.13   Robinson pressed rapidly ahead with his track-laying to complete the route to Hampton Court before Easter 1903.   Here the track is being put down in Kingston Road, Teddington.

2.14   Along the Hampton Court Road the double tracks are laid towards the Palace with the wall of Home Park behind.

2.15   This section of track along Hampton Court Road was the only part to have its roadway constructed of granite setts.

2.16   Outside the Livery & Bait Stables of the Kings Arms, Hampton Court. Having dug out the road to lay the tram track, the way ahead seems to require a lot of excavating.

2.17   Preparing the roadway outside the Lion Gate and the Kings Arms, north of Hampton Court Palace.

3. THREE DECADES OF TRAMWAY OPERATION

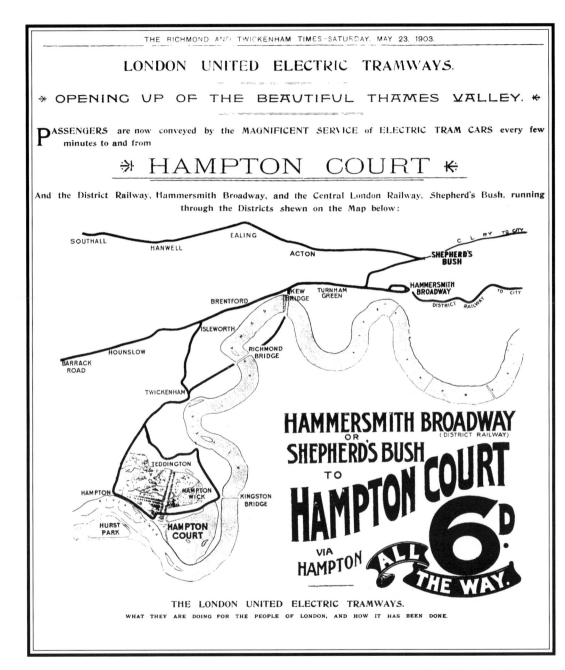

THE RICHMOND AND TWICKENHAM TIMES—SATURDAY, MAY 23, 1903.

LONDON UNITED ELECTRIC TRAMWAYS.

✷ OPENING UP OF THE BEAUTIFUL THAMES VALLEY. ✷

PASSENGERS are now conveyed by the MAGNIFICENT SERVICE of ELECTRIC TRAM CARS every few minutes to and from

✷ HAMPTON COURT ✷

And the District Railway, Hammersmith Broadway, and the Central London Railway, Shepherd's Bush, running through the Districts shewn on the Map below:

HAMMERSMITH BROADWAY
OR (DISTRICT RAILWAY)
SHEPHERD'S BUSH
TO
HAMPTON COURT
6D.
VIA HAMPTON ALL THE WAY.

THE LONDON UNITED ELECTRIC TRAMWAYS.
WHAT THEY ARE DOING FOR THE PEOPLE OF LONDON, AND HOW IT HAS BEEN DONE.

3.1   By the end of May 1903, London United Electric Tramways were advertising their frequent service of electric cars to Hampton Court.

3.2   Fulwell Depot as it appeared in 1905.

3.3   Inside Fulwell Depot, we can examine the detail of the wrought iron scroll work and the seating arrangements on the upper deck of the open topped cars.

3.4   Seats and trolley poles stretch into infinity.

3.5   Tram 289 has come over the railway bridge from Broad Street into the High Street, Teddington and is passing Elmfield House on the right where the great Russian philosopher, Alexander Herzen lived. Waldegrave Road is in the background.

3.6   The Tram terminus at Hampton Court Palace according to the postcard posted on 9th November 1903, with the tram on the left pausing on the spur line towards Hampton Court Bridge over the Thames.   It is ready to return to Richmond Bridge via Teddington while the tram on the right is preparing to return via Hampton to Hammersmith or Shepherds Bush.

3.7   This panoramic view of Hampton Court Tram Terminus from the Palace Gates towards Hampton Court Green shows cars 134, 83 and 284.

3.8   Tram 238, coming from Hampton Court past the Swiss Chalet by Tagg's Island, en route for Hammersmith in 1906 had to brave the regular floods in this stretch of the Hampton Court Road West.

3.9   Outside Garrick's Villa in Hampton, these four gaily bedecked trams have brought visitors to the house and grounds of the property lived in by Sir Clifton Robinson and his family.

3.10 Tram 252 rounds the corner of Hampton Court Road West into Church Street with the former public house 'The Feathers' to the left - it was the home of Hampton Historian, Henry Ripley - and Hampton's St. Mary's Parish Church to the rear. On the right can be easily discerned the single track that ran into the grounds of Garrick's Villa where Clifton Robinson parked a single deck saloon tramcar by means of which he could tour the system. When he was not using it, the tram could be hired for events and parties.

3.11 Mrs Elizabeth Seal who responded to my appeal in 1966 and allowed me to record her reminiscences of being a tram conductress from 1915 to 1919. She enjoyed her work even though there was a strict discipline. She lived near the Fulwell Depot whither she walked each morning from home. Her routes were mainly in the Kingston and Surbiton area. Even by 1966 much to everyone's dismay, she was happily jumping on and off the buses as she had done all those years before.

100m-11-27.

Form 510
Approved 31-5-20

THE LONDON UNITED TRAMWAYS, LIMITED.

Relief Way Bill Slip.

Time................................m.   Date........................192........

Car No.............................   Place.......................................

Route..............................   No............................UP DOWN

Starting No. from...

Tickets	Series	Starting No.	Finishing No.	Tickets	Series	Starting No.	Finishing No.
1d. C.							
1d.				4d. T.B.			
1½d.				5d. „			
2d.				6d. „			
3d.				7d. „			
4d.				8d. „			
5d.				9d. „			
6d.				10d. „			
7d.							
8d.				2d. W.R.			
9d.				3d. „			
10d.				4d. „			
11d.				5d. „			
1/-				6d. „			
				7d. „			
9d. Ch. Rt.				W.R. Ex.			
				Tfr. Ex.			
				Und. Ex.			
				Ch. Rt. Ex.			

Conductor................................   Badge No..................

3.12 LUET Relief Way Bill Slip.

3.13   The view of the depot from the Wellington Road entrance shows a mix of open top and closed top cars about 1924.

3.14   A remarkably good view of the interior length of the depot showing a line of ten cars plus others on the nearer tracks and original car 63 on route 67 destined for Hampton Court. This route number with minor alterations would remain in use for the next seventy years.

3.15   Clifton Robinson did not like closed top cars - perhaps a relic of his Bristol days - and it was only after he had resigned as managing director and chief engineer in 1910 that the Company began to add top covers to the upper deck although it never really began to protect its drivers from inclement weather until the advent of the Feltham car.   This tram was photographed in 1931 in Fulwell Depot ready for work on route 69.

3.16   By 1931 Fulwell was accepting trams from other undertakings with a view to their disposal. The tram on the left is LUT's. The works car (0)03 is probably LUT but the open top car may be SMET.   The fourth car looks like a Type U car.

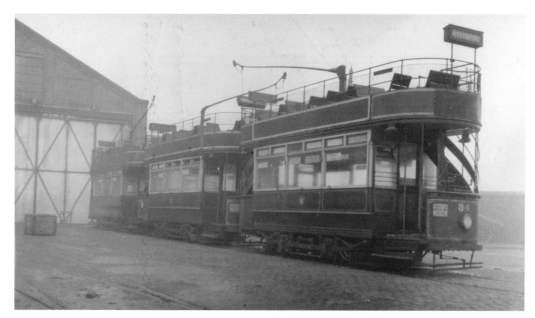

3.17 Three ex Croydon Corporation open top cars stand on the northernmost track on the Stanley Road end of Fulwell Depot in 1931.

3.18 Type Y double deck car enters the Wellington Road gates of the depot past the LUT offices. The sub-station is to the right.

3.19 Waiting for the change-over, three employees sit on the bench outside the Wellington Road gate to the depot.

**For other views of the tramways of the area,
see *Twickenham and Kingston Tramways*
*(Middleton Press).***

3.20   Car 255 is on single track outside the old Post Office in Hampton Hill bound for Hammersmith. There is a Prewett's Dairy hand-cart with milk-churn too close to the line to let the car proceed.

3.21   Double deck Car 277 runs on the double track in Hampton Hill on its way to Hammersmith. The cottages on the right still exist as does the greengrocer's on the left but the corner stationery and tobacco shop has become Hampton Hill Hardware.

3.22   Teaching recruits in 1934 at the Tramway Conductors' School, Acton. After studying the finer points of driving an electric tramcar, the trainees analyse the accident illustrated on the blackboard and then write a report.

3.23   Winnie Sinsbury's dad worked car 167 as its conductor from Fulwell on the 'Richmond Park Gates to Tolworth' route.

3.24   Mr T.J Dawson of 10 Lindum Road, South Teddington, a neighbour of my father-in-law, the
Scientific Instrument & Telescope Maker - R.N. Irving, also worked from Fulwell as the conductor
on car 240 on route 77.

3.25   By 1930 the trams were looking a bit tired and despite the addition of top covers and better
seating, the sparkle that had heralded their arrival thirty years earlier had gone. The pointsman in
front of the tram is using an original lever to change the points and there is still an open top car in the
shed.

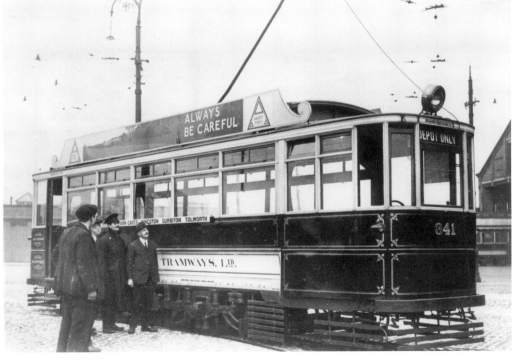

3.26   Despite a new tram bogie appearing on the depot tracks, the scene in 1931 against the wall backing onto the railway showed trams being broken up in the 'Bone-yard'.

3.27   In 1921the MET remodelled car 132 into a PAYE vehicle. It was later aquired by the LUT and renumbered 341. The one-man operator and the pay-as-you-enter scheme did not work well, only a further three trams being converted.

3.28   And trams still seemed to have a future, for after the amalgamation of all London's transport undertakings on July 1st 1933 into the hands of the London Passenger Transport Board, tram drivers in 1948 continued to be trained at the Clapham Depot where the Transport Museum was eventually set up for a while.

4. FULWELL STAFF CLUB AND INSTITUTE

4.1   Despite being a stickler for discipline and temperance among the LUT staff, Clifton Robinson also believed in providing them with a wide range of recreational facilities.   At Fulwell, between South Road and the northern side of the depot, an Association Football pitch (which became the cricket pitch in summer), a tennis court and a rifle range were laid out for the use of the staff.   On former allotments on the corner of South Road with Wellington Road, a large bowling green was created in 1956/7.

4.2   Just inside the Stanley Road entrance to the depot, a large building in the standard Fulwell style was designated for use of the staff as the Fulwell (London United Electric Tramway Ltd.) Club and Institute. It contained two full-size billiard tables.

4.3   The Company encouraged team games and indoor and outdoor competitions amongst the various depots. In 1903 the Clifton Robinson 'Tug of War' Challenge Cup was won by the Fulwell Depot Team consisting of Drivers Bingham, Seymour, Corry, Newman, Turner, Ireson, Gray, Hawkins and their coach: Driver How. They lost to the Hanwell Depot team the following year.

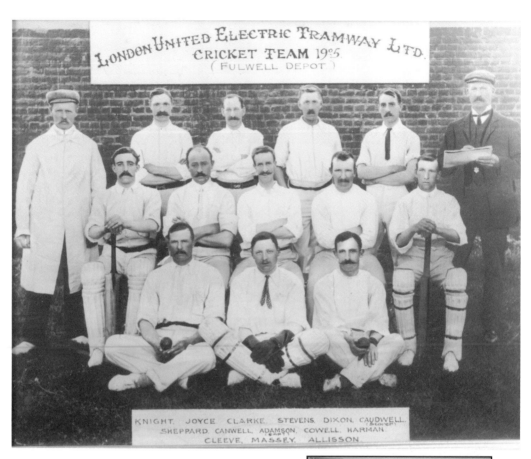

LONDON UNITED ELECTRIC TRAMWAY LTD.
CRICKET TEAM 1905
(FULWELL DEPOT)

KNIGHT. JOYCE. CLARKE. STEVENS. DIXON. CAUDWELL. (scorer)
SHEPPARD. CANWELL. ADAMSON. COWELL. HARMAN.
CLEEVE. MASSEY. ALLISSON.

4.4   Encouraged to play cricket, and Clifton Robinson led the way by having his own Garrick Cricket Club, the Fulwell Depot Cricket Team in 1905 was made up of Messrs. Knight, Joyce, Clarke, Stevens, Dixon, Caudwell (scorer), Sheppard, Canwell, Adamson (captain), Cowell, Harman, Cleeve, Massey, and Allisson.

L.U.T.

In Memory Of Our Comrades
Who Were Killed By Enemy Action
Fulwell Depot
1914–1918

C.Abbett	A.Crisp	J.heath	F.Millham
—.Alexander	C.Davis	C.hickey	A.Newman
h.Barley	G.Elsegood	J.Josling	J.Pollard
J.Bartlett	J.Ensome	W.Lucie	h.Randall
h.Blake	J.Fells	F.Maddison	C.Stephens
W.Chennells	C.Franks	J.Manby	S.Tasker
F.Cheney	C.hare	C.Massey	C.Thorpe
		G.Wooton	

1939–1945

O.Banyard	C.Charlkin	D.hunter	W.Pettit
h.Brewer	G.Davey	W.Jones	D.Russell
W.Bryant	W.Good	J.Maltby	A.Squires
		R.Warren	

Hounslow Depot
1914–1918

F.Bennett	h.Ellingham	A.Jones	G.Russell
		W.Webb	

1939–1945

A.Bich   L.Gomm

Memoria In Eterna

4.5   The memorial to those from the Fulwell and Hounslow Depots killed in the First and Second World Wars.

4.6   This portrait of Sister Janet Pearson hangs in a place of Honour inside the Fulwell Club.   She was a 'founder' member because she so carefully looked after the welfare of the drivers and conductors on the LUET when they stopped at the terminus outside her house on Kingston Hill. She always had a jug of tea or coffee ready for them and made sure they drank it! She listened to any worries and would offer her sympathetic advice. Lorna Cassidy remembers meeting her in Surbiton at an 'At Home' in Claremont Gardens in 1931-2 just before she died.

4.7   Sometimes there would be an outing from the depot for the male staff suitably dressed for the occasion to, let us say, Hampton Court.   In the photograph everyone is wearing a flower in his buttonhole so it must have been an important occasion.

4.8   Sometimes they would have hired a fleet of charabancs to take their families on an outing.

4.9   The LUT football club at Fulwell Depot won the Kingston & District Wednesday League in 1935-36. The team consisted of G. Sharpe, F. Ide, W. Roberts, W. Watson (goalkeeper), C. Maylings, J. Stevens, C. Brackley (manager), K. Young, J. Woods, T. Cassidy (captain), S. Ravenhill, R. Bolton.

4.10 LUT kiddies' outing in the 1930s. This picture is a souvenir from Winnie Sinsbury whose husband worked in the Fulwell works.

4.11 These three 'Clippies' formed the LUT table-tennis team. They attended their matches in uniform and always wore their 'bus' trousers and nice LUT shirts. Pat Piggott, not in uniform here, with her team-mates Betty Harwood and Daisy Collins, said that the team didn't do too badly in its first year but won the championship the following year in 1952/3.

4.12   The Fulwell Club had an outing to Wannock Gardens, Polegate, Sussex. Left to right: back row: Len Thorpe - Driver, Mr Kitchen - Garage Manager, Jim Dale - Union Rep, Dennis Boyd - Driver, Don Ruttie - Driver, Charlie Raven - Club Treasurer, Stan Piggott - 'general factotum' and did 'everything', Fred Nutting - Social Secretary. Front row: Mr. ? , Mrs Betty Thorpe, Pat Piggott - Clippie, Winnie Dale - Clippie, Mrs Raven, Mr Hall - Garage Manager after Mr Kitchen, Mrs Hall, Daisy Collins - Clippie, Mrs Nutting.

4.13   Fulwell Club Bowls Section in 1974 consisted of H. Mertens, F. Ide, A Owens, L. Hillier, J. Sims, and at the front B. Hill, B. Gleason, J. Stevenson, T. West, A. Piper, E. White, G. Mullins.

4.14   The Fulwell Depot (L.T.) Retired Members' Association Christmas Party, 1988.

4.15   Standing outside the Wellington Road garage exit these retired members are commemorating in 1992 the 30th Anniversary of the demise of the trolleybus.   The bus behind them is displaying the 667 route number, instead of the current 267. Frank Martingdale, Jack Clements, Jack Woolgar, John Curtin, Bill Baverstock (insp), George Dixon, Les Hughes, Alec Bowman, Albert Martin, Ron Hopkins, Tom Lazenby, Freddie Cromwell, Pat Piggott, Mrs Mick Gubbins, Arthur Williams.

4.16 TGW Union representative, Alan Moss and Trustee, Harry Mead, meet with the M.P. for Twickenham, Dr Vince Cable, and Cllr. Bryan Woodriff in August 2001 to highlight the problem with its lease that the Club was facing.

(Below and lower right) 4.17 Fulwell Depot (L.T.) Retired Members' Association, 2003 - the Gardening Section: (a) Reg Butler, George Costley, Joyce Dixon, Joan Costley, Winnie Piper, (b) Len Hedges, Lorna Cassidy, Jack Clements, Reg Butler, and Eileen Butler.

4.18   Backed up by their Trade Union Banner stating "Unity is Strength" the Fulwell Retired Members in 2001 faced an uncertain future with dignity, anger and hope.   Later the M.P. told the members they had won a valuable victory in securing a ten-year extension to their lease.   Let us hope that the reprieve will be used to ensure that the building will remain a Transport Members' club for many more years after that.   Peter Hendy, managing director of Transport *for* London expressed his recognition of the invaluable function the club performs for bus crews and retired staff in the area.

5. TRAM ASSEMBLY

5.1   The Underground Group, which included the LUT, had begun experimenting with new tramcar designs in the late twenties.   Prototypes were created at the Union Construction and Finance Company at its works in Feltham and were delivered to Fulwell for fitting out, painting and finishing. Experimental Feltham car 320 is at the UCC works awaiting transfer.

5.2   The Feltham cars were made on a lightweight all-metal chassis and framework.

5.3   This is the framework of No. 320.

5.4   The panels were fitted to the framework and the staircases formed an integral part of the structure.

5.5   The completed tram shell of one of the main production batch is depicted being towed on a specially-built low trailer behind a steam traction engine from Feltham to Fulwell.

5.6   At ten past four on 27th February 1931 the lights were switched on and the photographer, Hugh Nicol, made a remarkable picture of tracks 6 to 14 on the Wellington Road side with new Feltham car 358 on the main through line number 10. Car 58 is on line 7 and car 247 on line 12.

5.7   Two single-deck one-man trams used on the Brentford route with water car 002 were awaiting scrapping on 27th February 1931.

5.8   The completed experimental Feltham car awaits its finishing transfers at Fulwell.

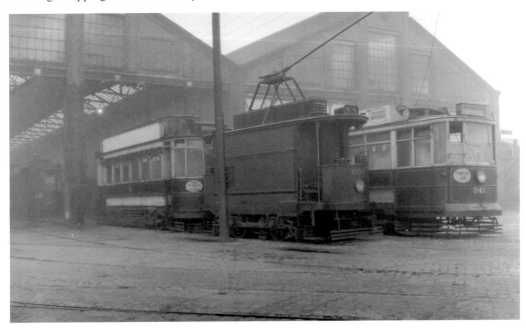

Vc 0709

DOWN	Fare	UP
Hampton Court		Park Road
Hampton Church	1d	StanleyRoad Junction
Uxbridge Road		Twickenh'm Fountain
Park Road		Twickenh'm (York Street Junction)
StanleyRoad Junction		Hill View Road
Twickenh'm Fountain		Isleworth Fire Station
Twickenh m (York Street Junction)		Bus Cor
Hill View Road		Syon Terrace
Isleworth Fire Station		Half Acre (brentfo-d)
Busch Corner		Kew Bridge
Syon Terrace		Gunnersb'ry Station
Half Acre (Brentford)		Turnham Gn Church
Kew Bridge		Young's Corner
Gunnersbury Station		Seven Stars
		Ravenscourt Park
Turnham Gn Church		Shepherds Bush
Depot		Hammers'ih

London United Tramways, Ltd.
Passengers must not break their journey. To be retained subject to which the passenger is issued subject to Co.'s Bye-laws.

5.9   Experimental Feltham car 330 is in Metropolitan livery at Fulwell but would new similar LUT trams give tramway operation from Fulwell a secure long-term future?

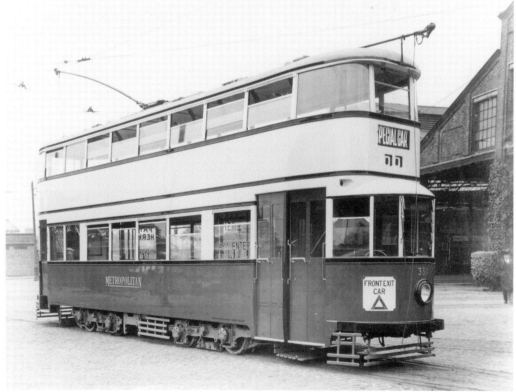

5.10   The advantages of the new vehicles can be seen in the next few pictures. The front end, left hand exit of a Feltham Car reflecting adjacent trams in Fulwell Depot.

5.11   The automatic doors and the pay-as-you-pass (enter) entrance of Feltham car 330. The production batch was configured traditionally without PAYE facilities.

5.12   The moquette upholstery and improved seating of the lower deck of the new Feltham cars.

5.13   The improved seating but more utilitarian upholstery of the upper deck.

6. THIRTY YEARS OF THE TROLLEYBUS

Planet News

TRACKLESS trams! This innovation to London appeared at Twickenham in May, 1931. The vehicle is built like a motor-bus, but draws its power from the overhead wire. It has, however, complete freedom of movement.

6.1   C.J. Spencer, the LUT General Manager believed strongly in the use of trams for heavily used routes but falling revenues in Twickenham and Kingston made the idea to use the new trolleybuses a very attractive proposition for the suburbs or smaller towns.   In September 1930, from the Stanley Road exit of Fulwell Depot a negative wire was strung alongside the positive over the tram route as far as the Church of St Peter and St Paul in Teddington's Broad Street and on 1st October an AEC trolleybus sealed the fate of the local tramways. Conversion took place piecemeal but trolleybus operations, the first in London, began on 16th May 1931 from Barclay's Bank in Twickenham as far as Teddington. Workmen can be seen carrying out further conversions to the overhead inside Fulwell Depot, while the trams still carry those passengers who need to travel beyond the current confines of the first London Trolleybus route.

6.2   An early plan of the Fulwell Depot site layout shows the disposition of the tramlines and the use to which the various buildings were put. Superimposed on the drawing is the way in which the depot is to adapt to accommodate both the trolleybuses and the trams.

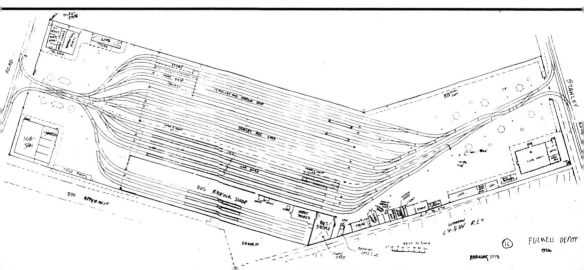

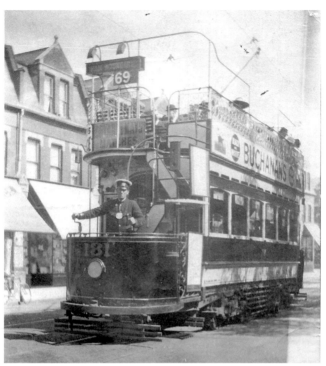

6.3   Until full conversion had been completed in November 1931, trams still had to be used.   Mr George Bournor drives the last LUT tram into Fulwell Depot on the shortened 69 route (Ham Boundary) via Stanley Road. Mrs Tagg, his daughter, said her father was born in 1876 and had joined the Company in 1903.

6.4   The Wellington Road/ Wellington Gardens corner of Fulwell Depot with no tram lines in the carriageway but fully set up for trolleybus operation.

6.5   Line of six Diddler Trolleybuses Nos. 3, 5, 53, 4, 6 and 2 await departure onto their new routes: 3 - The Dittons-Kingston Hill loop; 2 - Tolworth-Kingston Hill loop and 4 - Hampton Court-Wimbledon Station. Acquired from the UCC, the trolleybuses owe a lot of their design to the Feltham trams.

6.6   The line-up of five trolleybuses on the Wellington Road apron in October 1933 has the London transporT wording replacing the former London uniteD.

6.7   Four of the previous trolleybuses were photographed from a higher vantage point.

6.8   The five trolleybuses are viewed from the gateway into Wellington Road. The tramlines, the granite setts (cobbles) plus the LUT lamp on the gatepost are all still *in situ* but the old tram poles have been replaced by much stronger and less decorative ones.

6.9   Trolleybus training in 1934 at Fulwell on the Stanley Road apron involved attending to the trolley heads. Health and Safety would not permit nowadays the instructor to stand on the window frame outside the upper deck holding the trolley while the trainees dutifully observe.

6.10   On the same day in May the trainee learns how to reverse Diddler 19 by following the white line and keeping the rear wheels one foot away from it to learn 'turning in a restricted area'.

6.11   Trolleybus training on the practice bus.   The Driving Instructor has four trainees, one of which is in the driving seat.

6.12 SPECIAL Trolleybus 36 [NG 349] with the drivers taking a break during instruction on the road.

6.13 Staff still had to be smartly turned out at this time in the early 1930s.

6.14　A Diddler trolleybus on route 1, destined for Twickenham Junction is leaving the High Street, Teddington, to cross the Railway Bridge into Broad Street. Behind the trolleybus is the old Post Office. In the centre is the former Savoy Cinema and to the left is Elmfield House.

6.15　In the south west corner of the depot the workmen are seen overhauling the differential gears in 1937.

6.16   A long view of the General Shop at Fulwell Works in 1938 shows the layout of equipment and at the far end are a couple of trolleybuses.

6.17   The Fulwell Depot canteen is seen in 1947 with five Clippies having their cup of tea while two more wait at hatch 3/4 to be served.

6.18   The Ladies' Rest Room at Fulwell Depot in 1947.   Were there really only six comfortable upholstered seats for the Clippies?

6.19   From the Wellington Road entrance in 1954 one can see right through the garage to the trolleybuses on the Stanley Road apron.

6.20   The new trolleybuses had begun to arrive in 1935 and the trainees at the Fulwell Training School had to have the trolleybus contactors demonstrated to them.

6.21   At the Fulwell Works Paint Shop in 1937, the scaffolding employed by the men is of interest and they are painting the repaired trolleybus by hand.

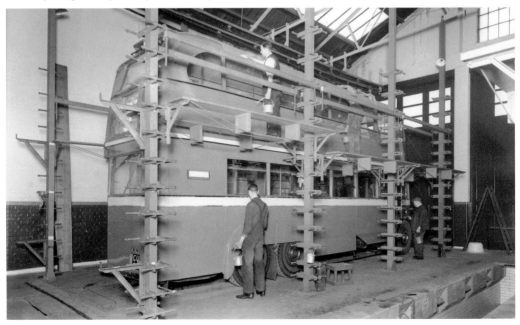

6.22   Trolleybus 84 is raised bodily above the pits in 1938 to allow for an inspection and overhaul of its motors etc.

6.23   Two Diddlers and three LT trolleybuses are in the 'Docking'/Stopping Pits being checked out in November 1937.

6.24   Trolleybus 88 [FW 15] has lost contact with the overhead wire and the driver, observed by the conductor, holds the long bamboo he has extracted from underneath the bus and tries to place the trolley head back on the wire.   The mishap occurred outside the Savoy Cinema in Teddington on route 601 from Tolworth to Twickenham.

6.25   James Vernon Payne AMIMechE
(1895-1958) was the Chief Electrical Engineer
who came down to Fulwell from London in
1930 to supervise the change-over from trams
to trolleybuses.   While at Fulwell he and his
wife first lived in Hibernia Road, Hounslow
but then moved to Ailsa Road just before the
War. He was offered the chance of moving to
Bristol as Chief Electrical Engineer but
declined the offer.

6.26   For the men who worked at Fulwell in
1938, they too had their own canteen although
there did not seem to be very much on the menu
that day.

6.27   Long-term LUT employee, Tom
Cassidy (1903 - 1983) worked his way
through several jobs from Tram Conductor
to Bus Driver on the 'little buses' to
Claygate.   As Union Secretary and
Representative   he   organised   a
countrywide raffle to raise enough money
to buy a TV set for the Convalescent Home
at Nettleport when TV sets were still a
rarity.   His widow, Lorna, was fated to
join the transport fraternity because when
she was quite young and living in
Kingston, she had the good fortune to be
scooped up by the 'lifeguard' on a passing
tram when she accidentally fell in front of
it.   She met Tom in 1930 and still has the
whistle he used on the open top trams to
instruct the driver to start or stop.

6.28   Eight new trolleybuses wait at the
Stanley Road gates in April 1938 for
dispatch to other depots.

6.29   Having seen Diddler No 1 pass through Kingston one lunch time in early May
1962 on its way to Fulwell Depot, I got permission from London Transport to visit the
Depot and take photographs of the trolleybus on the Stanley Road apron.

6.30   The controllers were very friendly and not only drove the trolleybus out for me to photograph that afternoon but allowed me to enjoy a special ride round the yard.

6.31   Watched by Mr A B B Valentine, the Chairman of LPTB, Ronald Hadland, conductor of the Diddler on the ceremonial run, hands a souvenir ticket to Mrs M B Davies, Mayor of Twickenham.

3.32   The Mayor of Malden & Coombe with Mr Valentine and Mr Robbins wait before the departure of Diddler No 1 on its ceremonial run.

6.33   On 8th May 1962 the children of St Mary's & St Peter's School in Teddington line the pavement outside their old school (Teddington Public Schools 1848) on the slope of Broad Street to the top of the railway bridge.   Broad Street shops are to the left and down Church Street to the right behind the school is the old Anglican Church of St Peter's & St Paul's. The pupils have turned out to see and cheer a trolleybus carrying guests on the official run over route 601.

6.34   Crowds of official visitors and enthusiasts watch the Diddler trolleybus set out on its special run from Stanley Road exit on the afternoon of May 8th 1962.

───────►

6.35   The police clear a path through the crowd as the last trolleybus to run in public service in London turns into Fulwell Depot after completing the final journey on route 604 from Wimbledon via New Malden (where I watched it), Kingston and Teddington.

───────►

6.36   The driver of London's official last trolleybus, Albert West congratulates his conductor, Ronald Gadsby of Fulwell on a job well done.   However, I have been told that Bill Brown, Dennis Hope's great uncle, actually drove the very last trolleybus into Fulwell Depot.

7. THE DIESEL BUS TAKES OVER

7.1   Late at night, the new Routemaster buses were lined up inside Fulwell Depot/Garage ready to spring into service on the morning after the last trolleybus had run. Ron Hadland drove the first Routemaster out of Fulwell Garage on May 9th 1962.

7.2   Club member Jack (Desmond) Clements at Twickenham Garage in 1954 dressed in his summer jacket and stands on the platform of an RT bus on route 27. Jack joined London Transport in 1947 and retired in 1986.

7.3   London Transport continued to use both sides of Fulwell depot for a while, but began to concentrate on the Wellington Road access. London Transport had set up this part of its empire as 'Cardinal District' with a small outline drawing of the bust of Cardinal Wolsey affixed to the outside of the buses. Two MCW Cardinal District buses on route 281 pass each other in front of Surrey County Hall in Penrhyn Road, Kingston.

7.4   The Stanley Road section was cut off and leased to Grundy, manufacturers of brewing equipment in the seventies. In 1986/7 the interior of the garage was altered transversely instead of lengthwise and the move cut off the Club and Institute from the busmen who continued to work the Wellington Road site. The site is precious for the future of public transport - buses or even new trams or trolleybuses.   It must not be lost to redevelopment but retained as an historical transport site and only developed as such.

8. LONDON UNITED BUSWAYS

8.1   London Transport privatised its services in 1994 and Cardinal District almost reverted to the original Company name of London United Busways.   A DT 74 rests on the forecourt of Fulwell Garage looking very small and lonely as if the two Metros in the background have shied away from it.

8.2   The sad millennium year scene is of neglect towards the old tram and trolleybus sheds to which London United Busways still needed access to accommodate and maintain its large fleet of buses. Many bus garages had been closed down.   In 1995, LUB took over Westlink at Kingston but lost the parking facility by the railway when the new bus station was built in Cromwell Road.

8.3   A Metro 16, commonly known as 'MI6', is bound for Fulwell Garage. It is at Hammersmith Butterwick just before route 33 stopped serving Queen's Gate, Kensington because of the new weight limit on Hammersmith Bridge.

8.4   Here is an example of London United's experimental livery which was not generally well received. It was mostly red, with cream around the top windows and blue/grey below hub level.

8.5   After route 33 was converted to single deck operation, DT 164 is seen at Wakefield Road, Richmond. Some were scheduled to do Richmond - Hammersmith 'shorts'.   Of note is the fact that DT 164 is carrying the old Routemaster registration number.

8.6   On 21st September 1997 at the Richmond Better Driving Day at the Rugby Football Union Ground in Twickenham, the Mayor of Richmond, my wife Cllr. Maureen Woodriff, was invited by London United Buses to be a 'Driver under instruction' in one of the training buses.   As always, the Company was keen to support local events.

8.7   DT 153 is parked in an almost empty garage at Fulwell so it must be a 'spread over' bus.

8.8   In its newly painted 'Hampton Court Palace' livery a DR 5 on route R68 waits outside Teddington Station.   Drivers generally preferred the DR 5 to the DT buses.

8.9   A London United DP 7 on route R70 bound for Hanworth and Hampton Nurserylands waits at the bus stop outside Fulwell Garage on Wellington Road.

8.10   Metro 1069, nicknamed the 'Belgrano', became the specially painted 'flagship' of the Company and did the rounds.   Here it is at a show displaying Shepherds Bush on route 88.

8.11   The special livery of Metro 1069 was a harking back to the former livery of London United Tramways.   The bus is outside the new bus station in Cromwell Road, Kingston with a few Westlink Titans in the background.

8.12   The Wellington Gardens end of Fulwell Garage and Leyland National LS 297 is being used for driver training.   These buses were fitted with the same engine and gearbox as Dennis Darts which made them a lot better.

8.13   When London United took over the 85 contract from Arriva, the buses came too.   Later they adopted the regular London United red and grey.

8.14   A row of five brand new TAs are on the forecourt at Fulwell with a Dennis Dart trying to look like one of the 'big boys'.

8.15   TA 231 stands waiting under the clock at Fulwell Garage, proving that vehicles may change but the backdrop does not.

8.16   John Gibney and Malcolm Claridge celebrate 100 years of 'London United' at Stamford Brook - the former Chiswick Depot - in front of a line-up of Routemasters (RMLs) on the 600 service to Tolworth in 2001.

8.17 One of three VRs (Volvo B7) at Hammersmith Bus Station in August 2002 setting off for Fulwell on the 267 route. They had been only recently introduced to the LUB fleet.

8.18 The now famous backdrop facing Wellington Road is used to its best effect, showing off a staggered row of LLWs ready for service on the Hounslow route 120. They were one of the first wheelchair accessible buses.

9. TELLINGS-GOLDEN MILLER

9.1   On 15th April 2000, Tellings Golden Miller Buses Ltd moved into the old tram/trolleybus depot on the Stanley Road site which gave it scope to expand its 14 local West London and Surrey bus routes and its coach operations.   Approaching the bus stop outside the Stanley Road entrance is Dennis Dart no. 429 (with Catano Nimbus engine) on route 465 for Fulwell Bus Depot.

9.2   In front of Reception is a Setra coach and a Dennis Dart (with Plaxton Pointer II) in the white, yellow and blue livery on route R70.   The old tramlines and granite setts had only just been concealed under a layer of tarmac to smooth out the surface of the forecourt.

9.3   Dennis Dart No 413 dedicated to the relatively new Hampton Court route R68, colourfully advertises its eventual destination.

9.4   Formerly the 'docking' area, now the 'pit' area with a StaRider by the windows; next is a green Mercedes Benz 709; a Dennis Dart with a Plaxton Pointer I and nearest the camera a full-size 12 metre Volvo B10 BLE (nicknamed Blobby) with Alexander - ALX 300 bodywork.

9.5   The panoramic view from above the buses in the garage pits of the Stanley Road forecourt and the Fulwell Club and Institute where T-GM drivers are welcome.

9.6   A Tellings-Golden Miller Dennis Dart and a Setra coach line up at the Stanley Road exit from the forecourt between the newly painted original gates and posts and the new signs on and above the old LUET Depot walls.

LONDON
UNITED

Fulwell Garage Centenary
1903 - 2003

Celebrating 100 Years of
Service to West London.

part of the

TRANSDEV
group

Middleton Press

Easebourne Lane, Midhurst, W Sussex. GU29 9AZ Tel: 01730 813169 Fax: 01730 812601
Email: enquiries@middletonpress.fsnet.co.uk   *If books are not available from your
local transport stockist, order direct with cheque, Visa or Mastercard, post free UK.*

BRANCH LINES

Branch Line to Allhallows
Branch Line to Alton
Branch Lines around Ascot
Branch Line to Ashburton
Branch Lines around Bodmin
Branch Line to Bude
Branch Lines around Canterbury
Branch Lines around Chard & Yeovil
Branch Line to Cheddar
Branch Lines around Cromer
Branch Line to the Derwent Valley
Branch Lines to East Grinstead
Branch Lines of East London
Branch Lines to Effingham Junction
Branch Lines around Exmouth
Branch Lines to Falmouth, Helston & St. Ives
Branch Line to Fairford
Branch Lines around Gosport
Branch Line to Hayling
Branch Lines to Henley, Windsor & Marlow
Branch Line to Hawkhurst
Branch Line to Ilfracombe
Branch Line to Kingsbridge
Branch Line to Kingswear
Branch Line to Lambourn
Branch Lines to Launceston & Princetown
Branch Lines to Longmoor
Branch Line to Looe
Branch Line to Lyme Regis
Branch Line to Lynton
Branch Lines around March
Branch Lines around Midhurst
Branch Line to Minehead
Branch Line to Moretonhampstead
Branch Lines to Newport (IOW)
Branch Lines to Newquay
Branch Lines around North Woolwich
Branch Line to Padstow
Branch Lines around Plymouth
Branch Lines to Princes Risborough
Branch Lines to Seaton and Sidmouth
Branch Lines around Sheerness
Branch Line to Shrewsbury
Branch Line to Swanage *updated*
Branch Line to Tenterden
Branch Lines around Tiverton
Branch Lines to Torrington
Branch Lines to Tunbridge Wells
Branch Line to Upwell
Branch Lines of West London
Branch Lines of West Wiltshire
Branch Lines around Weymouth
Branch Lines around Wimborne
Branch Lines around Wisbech

NARROW GAUGE

Branch Line to Lynton
Branch Lines around Portmadoc 1923-46
Branch Lines around Portmadog 1954-94
Branch Line to Southwold
Douglas to Port Erin
Douglas to Peel
Kent Narrow Gauge
Northern France Narrow Gauge
Romneyrail
Southern France Narrow Gauge
Sussex Narrow Gauge
Surrey Narrow Gauge
Swiss Narrow Gauge
Two-Foot Gauge Survivors
Vivarais Narrow Gauge

SOUTH COAST RAILWAYS

Ashford to Dover
Bournemouth to Weymouth
Brighton to Worthing
Eastbourne to Hastings
Hastings to Ashford
Portsmouth to Southampton
Ryde to Ventnor
Southampton to Bournemouth

SOUTHERN MAIN LINES

Basingstoke to Salisbury
Bromley South to Rochester
Crawley to Littlehampton
Dartford to Sittingbourne
East Croydon to Three Bridges
Epsom to Horsham
Exeter to Barnstaple
Exeter to Tavistock
Faversham to Dover
London Bridge to East Croydon
Orpington to Tonbridge
Tonbridge to Hastings
Salisbury to Yeovil
Sittingbourne to Ramsgate
Swanley to Ashford
Tavistock to Plymouth
Three Bridges to Brighton
Victoria to Bromley South
Victoria to East Croydon
Waterloo to Windsor
Waterloo to Woking
Woking to Portsmouth
Woking to Southampton
Yeovil to Exeter

EASTERN MAIN LINES

Barking to Southend
Ely to Kings Lynn
Ely to Norwich
Fenchurch Street to Barking
Hitchin to Peterborough
Ilford to Shenfield
Ipswich to Saxmundham
Liverpool Street to Ilford
Saxmundham to Yarmouth
Tilbury Loop

WESTERN MAIN LINES

Bristol to Taunton
Didcot to Banbury
Didcot to Swindon
Ealing to Slough
Exeter to Newton Abbot
Newton Abbot to Plymouth
Newbury to Westbury
Paddington to Ealing
Paddington to Princes Risborough
Plymouth to St. Austell
Princes Risborough to Banbury
Reading to Didcot
Slough to Newbury
St. Austell to Penzance
Swindon to Bristol
Taunton to Exeter
Westbury to Taunton

MIDLAND MAIN LINES

St. Albans to Bedford
Euston to Harrow & Wealdstone
St. Pancras to St. Albans

COUNTRY RAILWAY ROUTES

Abergavenny to Merthyr
Andover to Southampton
Bath to Evercreech Junction
Bath Green Park to Bristol
Burnham to Evercreech Junction
Cheltenham to Andover
Croydon to East Grinstead
Didcot to Winchester
East Kent Light Railway
Fareham to Salisbury
Frome to Bristol
Guildford to Redhill
Reading to Basingstoke
Reading to Guildford
Redhill to Ashford
Salisbury to Westbury
Stratford upon Avon to Cheltenham
Strood to Paddock Wood
Taunton to Barnstaple
Wenford Bridge to Fowey
Westbury to Bath
Woking to Alton
Yeovil to Dorchester

GREAT RAILWAY ERAS

Ashford from Steam to Eurostar
Clapham Junction 50 years of change
Festiniog in the Fifties
Festiniog in the Sixties
Festiniog 50 years of enterprise
Isle of Wight Lines 50 years of change
Railways to Victory 1944-46
Return to Blaenau 1970-82
SECR Centenary album
Talyllyn 50 years of change
Wareham to Swanage 50 years of change
Yeovil 50 years of change

LONDON SUBURBAN RAILWAYS

Caterham and Tattenham Corner
Charing Cross to Dartford
Clapham Jn. to Beckenham Jn.
Crystal Palace (HL) & Catford Loop
East London Line
Finsbury Park to Alexandra Palace
Holbourn Viaduct to Lewisham
Kingston and Hounslow Loops
Lewisham to Dartford
Lines around Wimbledon
Liverpool Street to Chingford
London Bridge to Addiscombe
Mitcham Junction Lines
North London Line
South London Line
West Croydon to Epsom
West London Line
Willesden Junction to Richmond
Wimbledon to Beckenham
Wimbledon to Epsom

STEAMING THROUGH

Steaming through Cornwall
Steaming through the Isle of Wight
Steaming through Kent
Steaming through West Hants

TRAMWAY CLASSICS

Aldgate & Stepney Tramways
Barnet & Finchley Tramways
Bath Tramways
Brighton's Tramways
Bristol's Tramways
Burton & Ashby Tramways
Camberwell & W.Norwood Tramways
Clapham & Streatham Tramways
Croydon's Tramways
Dover's Tramways
East Ham & West Ham Tramways
Edgware and Willesden Tramways
Eltham & Woolwich Tramways
Embankment & Waterloo Tramways
Exeter & Taunton Tramways
Fulwell - Home to Trams, Trolleys and Buses
Great Yarmouth Tramways
Greenwich & Dartford Tramways
Hammersmith & Hounslow Tramways
Hampstead & Highgate Tramways
Hastings Tramways
Holborn & Finsbury Tramways
Ilford & Barking Tramways
Kingston & Wimbledon Tramways
Lewisham & Catford Tramways
Liverpool Tramways 1. Eastern Routes
Liverpool Tramways 2. Southern Routes
Liverpool Tramways 3. Northern Routes
Maidstone & Chatham Tramways
Margate to Ramsgate
North Kent Tramways
Norwich Tramways
Reading Tramways
Seaton & Eastbourne Tramways
Shepherds Bush & Uxbridge Tramways
Southend-on-sea Tramways
South London Line Tramways 1903-33
Southwark & Deptford Tramways
Stamford Hill Tramways
Twickenham & Kingston Tramways
Victoria & Lambeth Tramways
Waltham Cross & Edmonton Tramways
Walthamstow & Leyton Tramways
Wandsworth & Battersea Tramways

TROLLEYBUS CLASSICS

Croydon Trolleybuses
Derby Trolleybuses
Hastings Trolleybuses
Huddersfield Trolleybuses
Maidstone Trolleybuses
Portsmouth Trolleybuses
Reading Trolleybuses
Woolwich & Dartford Trolleybuses

WATERWAY ALBUMS

Kent and East Sussex Waterways
London to Portsmouth Waterway
West Sussex Waterways

MILITARY BOOKS

Battle over Portsmouth
Battle over Sussex 1940
Blitz over Sussex 1941-42
Bombers over Sussex 1943-45
Bognor at War
Military Defence of West Sussex
Military Signals from the South Coast
Secret Sussex Resistance
Surrey Home Guard

OTHER RAILWAY BOOKS

Index to all Middleton Press stations
Industrial Railways of the South-East
South Eastern & Chatham Railways
London Chatham & Dover Railway
London Termini - Past and Proposed
War on the Line (SR 1939-45)

BIOGRAPHY

Garraway Father & Son